JESUS

The Final Hours

Michael

WestBow Press books may be ordered through booksellers or by contacting:

WestBow Press
A Division of Thomas Nelson
1663 Liberty Drive
Bloomington, IN 47403
www.westbowpress.com
1-(866) 928-1240

Because of the dynamic nature of the Internet, any web addresses or links contained in this book may have changed since publication and may no longer be valid. The views expressed in this work are solely those of the author and do not necessarily reflect the views of the publisher, and the publisher hereby disclaims any responsibility for them.

Any people depicted in stock imagery provided by Thinkstock are models, and such images are being used for illustrative purposes only.

Certain stock imagery © Thinkstock.

ISBN: 978-1-4497-7676-3 (sc)
ISBN: 978-1-4497-7677-0 (e)

Library of Congress Control Number: 2012922042

Printed in the United States of America

WestBow Press rev. date: 01/14/2013

TABLE OF CONTENTS[1]

---

1 To the Reader, It should be noted that in this Poem some lines are Acrostic, i.e., the First letter of the First word that begin these lines is separated by a space from the next letter(s) of the same word, e.g., **J ESUS** instead of **JESUS**. When many Acrostic lines appear together, the First letter of each consecutive Acrostic line spells out a Biblical Verse which underscores the meaning of the Poem. All of the First letters that make up these Acrostic verses have been highlighted.
AUTHOR.

The Acrostics:

DAN 9:26 - And after threescore and two weeks shall Messiah be **CUT OFF,** but not for himself.

ISA 53:8 - He was **CUT OFF** out of the land of the living: for the transgression of my people was he stricken.

THE SECOND GARDEN

DRAMATIS PERSONAE

JESUS, The Son of GOD.

The Disciples of JESUS } Peter,

} John,

} James.

Michael, The Prince of the children of Israel.

Satan, as the Scapegoat & Dragon.

THE SCENE: Gethsemane.

PART I

JESUS - The Disciples:

Peter, Peter, dwellest upon the sleeve? [1]

Even these stones with dewey drops grieve.

Mainstay these brothers; kneeled-petitions plead,

Mine sorrow laboreth in the worst degree. –

Endure this hour which for a moment is here;

For, lo, the Forces of the Night draw ominously near. -

Knowest not yet the sentinels bitter end?

Tis Sleep!, Sleep!, Death's cajoling, charm'ed friend.

Guilt-shamed, abashed, all a-flush, blanched-grey,

Faulting the other, each reproaches inveighs; -

But their sleepy awareness and sheepish chagrin,

Make these random excuses seem flaccid and thin.

And as they rub their worn eyes, and half-stiffened limbs,

He bids them be vigilant and stay wakeful for him.

Thence wandering away, lost, returning he crept:

A distraught sigh of distracted step. –

---

1 MAT 26:36-44; MRK 14:32-40; LUK 22:39-46.

Fading slowly from sight; into Olivet's thick maze;

(A darkened retreat for one trapped and half-crazed),

As The Man flees the light; he senses his death,

For he sees in each shadow some presence or threat:

Some skulking Silohuette; some Specter that stirs,

(Half-something, half-nothing, half-image, half-blur).

By his dread of the morrow, he's unnerved and unhinged,

Causing courage to cower and conviction to cringe,

And as he veers toward the clearing known only for prayer;

(Now bathed in pale moonbeams of the bright lunar glare)

Under Nisan's Pasch-eye, like a lamb to be sheared, [2]

His anguish bewails his rising sorrows and fears:

O comfort me Father, O comfort thy Son,

Un-bend thy firm will, and let the Comforter come.

Mine eye runneth down with the waters of grief, [3]

For the Comforter is far and extends no relief.

My sighs have increased, and my heart is too faint,

Mine enemies have gathered, and show no restraint.

Why hold my life forfeit?, and in sacrifice expend?

Re-weigh the Sin-balance, and thy Judgement suspend.

Pray remember what further is yet to be done,

And consider the works which we've only begun:

---

2 **EST 3:7(Nisan) or EXO 13:3-4(Abib).**
N.B.1 – The First month of the Biblical Year.
N.B.2 – Pasch(Pesach) refers to Passover.
AUTHOR.
3 **LAM 1:16-17.**

Blest are the Poor, whose spirits have quickened,[4]

Blest are the Mournful, whose hearts were once Stricken.

Blest are the Meek, whose inheritance is sure,

Blest are the Truthful, who all guile deplore.

Blest are the Merciful whom thy mercy pursues,

Blest are the Pure, who seeing ME, have seen YOU.

Blest are the Children who light up our lives,

Blest are the Righteous, who for righteousness strive,

Blest are the Men who repent and are shrived...

The quiet that follows is filled with unrest,

But the Garden is deaf, and hears not his distress.

A soft gentle breeze stirs the ungentle night,

But the Garden is mute and speaks not to his plight.

The Moon overhead marks its zenith and place,

But the Garden is blind and looks not on his face;

For this Garden is Eden, which bars the Earth-race.

Un-answered, un-seen, un-heard and un-manned,

His seething hurt-pride into anger expands.

Matching equal contempt with ignoring insult,

His temper explodes into a ranting tumult:

---

4 **MAT 5:3-10.**

If vengeance be the key which opes thy locked-heart,

Then conflate my Two Comings and perform the last part.

Let this Cup be removed; let its contents be shared,

Let Justice prevail, and let no one be spared.

Let all who have trespassed in action or doubt,

Drink their fair portion til this Vial's poured out.

As soon as this tirade had roared through his lips,

The Man quickly prayed that his rage be dismissed.

With no one to hear, and the night for a friend,

He paces and paces without purpose or end.

Then comes a small stillness; (which none might disturb) –

Til a sound of a going in the tree-tops is heard. [5]

As the air seems to thicken; into contour and form,

Out of nothing some someone comes shaped and adorned:

(Though his figure and trace were of Angelic design,

His similitude bore feature to the A-dam-ic line,)

And in one fluid movement he before The Man stands,

Like one in obedience heeds a spoken command.

---

5 **1 CHR 14:15.**

PART II

Out of deference he waits; in stiff-martial repose,

For the sign which will bid him his purpose expose.

With his presence acknowledged, he his presence pursues,

In a language unknown since the World first renewed:

Angel – JESUS:

T welve legions have rallied at this Star-system's edge, [6]

H ailed by the Watchers; who never doubt or allege, [7]

E xclaiming devotion to The Man who is pledged.

Pausing, then abruptly,

L et my Lord but decree, and in the LIVING-GOD'S name:

O rder these pure-warriors to punish the blamed.

R everse the course-promised; twas given good run,

D eclare the next stage, and undo what's begun!

The vehemence and swiftness of the Angel's outburst,

Overwhelms The Man greatly, and he fears for the worst.

Like a statue transfixed in cold-marble and square:

(With posture fixed rigid, and blank-vacant stare),

He clearly surmises what his torment expressed,

As a blind sudden panic creeps into his breast.

With controlling emotion he in earnestness speaks,

Reproving himself lest blind-havoc be wreaked:

---

6 This is the First Acrostic(Michael): **The Lord is my shepherd - PSA 23:1.**
N.B.1 - Because of the dialogue between Michael and JESUS, their Acrostics interplay and should be followed respectively.
AUTHOR.
7 **DAN 4:13-27.**

JESUS – Angel:

H ath the ALMIGHTY declared, 'Let My Will be un-done, [8]

E rase the Writ-Promise if it pleases my Son?' –

Pausing,

I saiah never stated in the Scripture of Truth: [9]

S lay Satan's-scapegoat; spare the Sin-substitute.

B arren Elizabeth, when her husband was told, [10]

R ejected any fears, though her years were old, -

O bserve how my mother; more a daughter back then,

U nsure of a conception deemed impossible by men,

G ave trusting consent; only to brave every slight,

H eartrending good-Joseph by her un-wedded sight,

T ill neither could tell what was wrongful or right.

A re they now to ponder if their sacrifice was vain?

S hall I ask an exemption when they ne'er complained?

A nd; 'Who is like GOD', who can Prophecy change?

Michael – JESUS:

I n answer to the query which addresses by Name; [11]

S ay rather his Word rests in mercy un-feigned. –

---

8 This is the Second Acrostic(JESUS): **He is brought as a lamb to the slaughter - ISA 53:7.**
9 **ISA 53:4-5; LEV 16:8-10.**
10 **LUK 1:5-25.**
11 **Michael.** 4317 Miyka'el me-kaw-ale' from 4310 and (the prefix derivative from) 3588 and 410; **WHO (IS) LIKE GOD?**; Mikael, the name of an archangel and of nine Israelites:--Michael. **STRONG'S CONCORDANCE.**

Pausing,

M ixed message attended thy statements afore;

Y ielding convictions make thy Servants un-sure.

JESUS – Michael:

L et my Watchers know this; that by all that's foresworn,

A damant am I – and for this purpose I'm born…

M ake thou one gesture more ere thou finally depart -

B e thou prayerful with me, and in an old song take part:

JESUS:

S trangers and sojourners since the dawning of time[12],

Michael:

H elpers and shepherds in El-o-him's design. [13]

JESUS:

E den's belov'ed, once in-separate, was torn;

Michael:

P arted and longed for as a Spouse that is mourned.

JESUS:

H eaven lamented; though her children were cross,

Michael:

E xpending her Prophets to recover her loss

JESUS and Michael:

R emember, O LORD, and let their memory abide,

---

12 **LEV 25:23.**
13 **THE LIVING GOD.**
430 'elohiym el-o-heem' plural of 433; gods in the ordinary sense; but specifically used (in the plural thus, especially
with the article) of the supreme God; occasionally applied by way of deference to magistrates; and sometimes
as a superlative:--angels, X exceeding, God (gods)(-dess, -ly), X (very)great, judges, X mighty. **STRONG 'S**
CONCORDANCE.

D eclare the true Bridegroom, and make thy City his Bride.

As their singing subsides; these two Beings from afar,

In honoring their roles, will be covered with scars.

But the Hour is fleeting; he must now underway:

His presence is crucial in the upcoming days.

So with one firm salute, he ascends the Star-heights,

Til his Soul disappears past the orbiting lights.

PART III

For a time The Man stared; then his eyes turned away,

Recalling a Garden from a long ago day:

A Garden where all who were fashioned began;

Fleshed out of the Earth; (where GOD planted The Man),

A Garden whose glory the Sons of GOD praised, [14]

Until the Enemy entered and shortened his days... [15]

He grieves in his mind, and seeks solace in prayer,

Yet that Garden persists, changing hope to despair. -

His old fears return; they're now stronger than he,

He cannot forget, though he the Son of GOD be.

In agony-severe; in violent tremulous shakes,

Bloody-sweat beads and falls with each spasm and quake.

Thus wracked in his soul, and un-ravelled in mind,

He flees from the light into Mount Olive's design -

To the place where The Three still in slumber have lain;

When a lone voice starts wailing of a debt un-reclaimed.

From a faraway distance he discerns a faint step;

(Like a hollowed-out echo in a canyon or depth).

Its slow steady pace seems to rhytmically tap

As it wends through the darkness in which it is trapped. -

Its the one always freed, into banishment driven, [16]

---

14 **JOB 38:1-7.**
15 **GEN 6:3.**
16 **LEV 16:21-22.**

13

Whose Annual-Exile meant the Tribes were forgiven.

Now its perennial wan'dring heeds GOD'S awful beck,

As a death-tolling bell dangles from that goat's neck.

Here the Pasch and Atonement come full circle round, [17]

And for once their united and integrally wound.

Toward the trespassing line where his edge meets our side,

He awaits the command to begone or abide.

The Garden's transformed, it is dark all around,

And he and his adversary in this vision are wound.

In nightmare and real-time shall this battle be pitched;

Til this Passover ends - fulfilled or be-witched. -

No dialogue's exchanged - no condition's requested,

The gauntlet's been thrown and with a gaunt look accepted.

Without further regard, he o'erleaps the purlieus,

And shape-shifts his image as he steps into view.

In garb like a Harlequin who postures and mimes

To a Minstrel's mute-flute piping silence in time,

He dances and prances and frolics and skips,

As his countenance darkens and a sneer curls his lips -

(Like a Sadist or Gaoler will his victim torment,

So he hummeth that Psalm with its dire portent.) [18]

With cold-lifeless eyes he keenly probes and discerns;

Cir'cling and spinning as he mockingly turns.

---

17 The dynamics surrounding this Passover will be discussed in a future work. **AUTHOR.**
18 **PSA 22:14-18.**

Winding closer and closer, he trip-ping-ly hops,

Til their eyes lock and level and he suddenly stops...

Through the unspoken word, and the all-telling glance:

There's nothing to say, and there's nothing to chance.

His sparring has ended, and both are resigned;

Now this Battle must enter the next level in Time...

His strategy is simple - their will be an Exemption:

Exchange his own Scapegoat for the one of Redemption.

Undo this damned-Prophecy by default and Pre-emption! [19]

With a wink and a leap he quickly slips out of sight,

As reality returns to the sounds of the night...

---

19 **DAN 7:25c.**
N.B.1 – Exemption: a freedom or release from an existing liability or obligation.
JESUS was obligated by the **ISA 53:8** and **DAN 9:26a** Prophecy(s) to forfeit His life as a Passover-offering.
A Passover-offering was to be without blemish – **LEV 12:5.**
N.B.2 – Pre-emption: to prevent or delay an intended action from taking place, or to undo its purpose.
Jesus Bar-abbas was intended as a substitute sacrifice that would have polluted the **ISA 53:8** and **DAN 9:26a** Prophecy(s).
N.B.3 – Satan's policy was and still is 'to change the Prophetic Times and the Laws of GOD'. The logic within the Kingdom of Hell, then as well as now, would have been: **IF WE CAN UNFULFILL JUST ONE PROPHETIC-STEP, THEN WE CAN UNFULFILL ALL THE PROPHECY(S) THAT SPEAK OF OUR OWN DAMNATION.**
AUTHOR.

PART IV

Sans warning, strange lightnings and thunders uproar,

As the Earth gapes and widens to reveal its black-maw.

Out of deep-hidden cellars; (more like Coffins in Graves),

Come blood-curd'ling howls, and banschee death-raves.

From that un-sounded Pit issues an Image-Grotesque;

Multi-headed in form and complete martial dress:

Battle-clad, and War-panoplied; in wrought-armor arrayed,

He stalks and he threatens in ever mounting displays.

Then closing the distance in one mighty bound,

He forges his Hate into these menacing sounds:

Satan(as Dragon) – JESUS:

T wilight for the gods is darker than dark,[20]

H ell opes its hot-furnace to receive thy last spark;

E ternal damnation awaits those I have marked.

L ook back to the days when the Babylonian hordes

O verran thy GOD'S temple with base fire and sword.

R ecidivism be-deviled thy transgressing ilk;

D eserved not cursed-Canaan their honey and milk?

Pausing,

H ow goes the line-chosen?, Is the Messiah on time?

A re thy Scryers well-proven?, or is thy word too sublime?

T *hy* GOD told that Harlot she would trample *my* seed; [21]

H ath my brow any bruise, or does *her* heel sorely bleed?

---

20 This is the Third Acrostic(Satan): **The Lord hath forsaken the earth and the Lord seeth not - EZK 9:9.**
21 **GEN 3:15.**

Pausing,

F ollow now a Creation easily bent by my hand:

O ffending their Deity, the Twin-breeders were banned. [22]

R ejecting their kind; into Perversions were led, [23]

S kin-species Trans-mixed; and under my plan they bred.

A berrations soon marred Ante-Diluvia's blueprint,

K ulling out the last traces of the Original hint.

E volution?, or mutation?, it was all so un-fitted,

N o solution was found - *YOUR* **GOD WAS OUTWITTED!**

Pausing,

T heir design was deep-flawed - (an Omniscient mistake!),

H uman and Divine can not be one or cognate. -

E xiled are those who will dare Incarnate.

Pausing,

E xpect neither rescue nor Resurrection when dead;

A s if Bethany's son from the underworld was led. [24]

R ather think, and consider; for thy next actions' geared:

T he powers-provoked will in force soon appear.

H ear the option-provided, which will all charges clear:

A n Alternate's been chosen; Bar-abbas surnamed,

N one shall deny that for sedition he's blamed;

D ecide ere the order for thy capture is framed.

---

22 **Adam**(The Man) and **Adam**(The Woman).
GEN 2:21-24; GEN 5:1-2.
23 **GEN 6:1-13.**
24 **JHN 11:1-46; JHN 12:1-11.**

Pausing,

T wilight for the gods is darker than dark.

H ere it will end without note or remark.

E xchange thy lead-role and accept my bit-part.

L et My Firstborn be chosen; (he is also despised),

O ffered and switched, like a Changeling disguised -

R equired only this; (by Bel-te-shaz-zar's timeline):

D eliver a Messiah after three-score and nine. [25]

Pausing,

S on of the Father? - who's to care by what god,

E xpiate High Caiaphas and court Pilate's nod.

E xpatriate thyself to where Rome lays no claim:

T hules a safe-haven to seek honor and fame - [26]

H eroics oft end in humiliating shame.

Pausing, then angrily:

N othing shall be altered by the fact *you* were born,

O verrated in death by those you've suborned -

T he Preterists shall prove that your story's well-Worn.

Con-tu-me-lious fumings now escape from his lips;

(Like sounds-inarticulate from a choking handgrip),

But ere this Behemoth presumes to trample about,

Within his minds-eye, The Man motions him out.

And in departing he hears; whom he slandered with lies,

The Man pledge his life, a prey, ransom, and prize.

---

25 **DAN 9:26a.**

26 Ultima Thule, furthest Thule, an island placed by Ancient Geographers North of the British Isles; hence, any far-distant, unknown land. **LITTLE AND IVES UNIVERSAL DICTIONARY.**

PART V

JESUS(Soliloquy):

T hou, O Woman's Seed, who art ever by my side, [27]

O ver Eden's threshold shall be carried as my Bride.

T wo hearts shall embrace, without Time-interrupt,

H ephzibah shalt thou be, when I thee lift up. - [28]

E nter Beulah with me, where the Angelic-ones sup.

In that one final sigh he breathes out his last fear,

As resolve steels his heart; (for the morrow draws near).

Looking round one more time; he is flushed and inspired,

But there's nothing to show of what had lately transpired:

For this Garden's absorbed what had warred in his Soul,

Now *it* seems deserted, and ***his*** Spirit is whole.

As The Three figures sleeping have not wakened or stirred;

(Though the Furies of Hell about their dreams whirred)

He espies at a distance; a faint outline of men,

Whose marching presages his long-journey's end.

Into Hostility's arms he's now fatally thrust,

As he utters the words that will condemn him to dust:

---

27 **GEN 3:15; REV 12:1-6; REV 19:6-9.**
28 **ISA 62:4.**

S eize the Pasch-Lamb, and anoint the cursed-tree,

L et the High-Priest cast lots and Azazel set free.[29]

A llow this sin-off'ring; and this epitaph append:

U nconditional love lays down its life for its friends.

G reater burden of proof I cannot conceive;

H enceforth shall The Woman en-compass her Seed. [30]

T o her Womb shall her own return in due time,

E voking this sacrifice as a testament and sign.

Looking on the Three Disciples

R est ye now and sleep on - I am faithfully resigned.

....

All around, all around, all, all, around,

The hissing is circling, the hissing surrounds.

Awful cursings and screechings race here and about

As that blaspheming chorus breaks up into shouts,

And the trailing of voices begin to disperse

Into hue-cries and torches that purposely search.

---

29 **LEV 16:8-10, 20-22.**
Azazel.
5799 `aza'zel az-aw-zale' from 5795 and 235; goat of departure; the scapegoat:--scapegoat. **STRONG 'S CONCORDANCE.**
30 **JER 31:22.**

THE TRIAL

DRAMATIS PERSONAE

JESUS, the Son of GOD.

Simon Peter, a disciple of JESUS.

The Eleven disciples & Judas Iscariot.

Captain of the Guards.

Annas, father-in-law of Caiphas.

The Disciple.

Caiaphas, the High-Priest.

Pilate's wife.

Satan, as the King of the Gods.

Pontius Pilate, the Prefect of Judaea.

Messenger to Pilate.

Herod Antipas, the Tetrarch of Galilee & Perea.

Herodias, the wife of Antipas.

Jesus Bar-Abbas.

Legio, the Chorus.

Guards, Elders, Scribes, Servants, Officers, Soldiers, etc.

PROLOGUE

F our men would be hanged, and the Fifth would be freed, [1]

O n the day they debuted, twas a tale of Two Seeds,

R ehearsed from pre-birth for the roles they'd fulfill,

H ere they'll perform by command of Divine Will.

E ach one of the cast for past-actions were seized,

T hread into a plot which High-Prophecy had weaved;

H ow deft was that pen when the Playwrite of Time,

A ctors appointed, and accusations assigned.

T he conspiracy began as the Psalmist portrayed; [2]

I n Infamy's roll, with the one who betrayed:

S ole scion of Simon - like that Nabal of old, [3]

H exed straight from a womb often bartered and sold.

A dept with the purse, he assumed full possession,

N or spake there a voice choosing Levi's profession. [4]

G uided by zealot, Messianic-like visions,

E xploited was he for another's ambition.

---

1 This is the First Acrostic: **For he that is hanged is accursed of GOD - DEU 21:23.**
2 **PSA 41:5-9.**
3 **JHN 12:4; 1 SAM 25:2-3.**
4 **Matthew the disciple.**
MAT 9:9, MAR 2:14; LUK 5:27.

D esigned were the parts for the Two malcontents, [5]

I n spite of their crimes they were Two temperments.

S taked were they both near the tree in the midst – [6]

A s two signs in a road pointing that way or this.

C rook'd was the course for the one of pure wrath,

C oarse-footed the way for the troubled-man's path,

U nderstudy's for both would from thence unto hence

R eprise the twin roles that reject and repent.

S tranger than fiction was the Truth in the end,

E ntailing a law which mob-justice would bend –

D enounced by a Custom not of Rome or the Jews, [7]

O ne JESUS was sentenced - One Jesus excused. [8]

F rom Gab-ba-tha's mouth spake the High-Sadducee, [9]

G OD'S hand in man's glove signed the mutual decree.

O f the Five who were billed, only one walked away,

D eferred as a sequel that will read in our day.

---

5 **ISA 53:9.**
6 **MAT 27:38-44; MRK 15:27; LUK 23:32-33; JHN 19:16-18.**
7 **MAT 27:15; MRK 15:6; LUK 23:17; JHN 18:39.**
8 **JESUS the CHRIST / Jesus Bar-Abbas.**
N.B.1 - 912.Barabbas bar-ab-bas of Chaldee origin ((1347 and 5); son of Abba; Bar-abbas,an Israelite:--Barabbas. **STRONG 'S CONCORDANCE.**
N.B.2 - Barabbas' name appears as *bar-Abbas* in the Greek texts. It is derived ultimately from the Aramaic, *Bar-abba*, 'son of the father'. According to early Greek texts, Barabbas' full name was *Jesus Barabbas*. Later texts shorten his name to just *Barabbas*. **WIKIPEDIA.**
9 **JHN 19:13-15.**

ACT I
SCENE 1: The Garden of Gethsemane.
The 14th of Nisan(about Midnight).

A lone and abandoned, with no friend to entreat, [10]

W rested from judgement by brute-force and deceit,

A bducted by wolves in the guise of sheeps clothes,

K issed and embraced by a Miser that lothes,

E xacting the price which was long since foretold, [11]

O ur Shepherd was taken when the night air was cold...

S imon rose first, with sword brandished in hand, [12]

W ielding its length, he maimed one of the band.

O thers half-hearted; rough-rousted from sleep,

R esisting the mob were soon tossed in a heap.

D etained and encircled, they are herded like sheep.

A ccosting The Twelve, the armed-vanguard inspects,

G auging what face may their status reflect.

A waiting their Chief, they the company demand,

I dentities of each; but defiant they stand. -

N ext onto the scene struts a bully and scowler,

S hoving the captives, and branding them prowlers,

T elling them tersely of his purpose and power.

---

10 This is the Second Acrostic: **Awake, O sword, against my shepherd, and against the man that is my fellow, ... smite the shepherd, and the sheep shall be scattered - ZEC 13:7.**
11 **ZEC 11:12-13.**
12 **MAT 26:51; MRK 14:47; LUK 22:50; JHN 18:10.**

M inutes elapse, and then the order's made clear:

Y ield up the false-Christ, or risk judgement-severe!

S ilence prevails as the moon gloats and glowers,

H arrowing the moment, and exploiting the hour;

E xpiring-patience, and Im-po-tent-rage,

P ersuade the vexed-Captain to confront and engage.

H astening a guard who disappears from the scene,

E xchanges are heard; they are harsh and obscene,

R eturning, the guard, with another, keeps pace -

D eceptive deep shadows have cloaked his marked face.

A dvancing sheep-like toward The One in the midst,

N earing The Man he notes the clenching of fists.

D iscerned by them all - he betrays with a Kiss. [13]

A ngry hot curses pour from out the held-group;

G rapplings and scufflings surprise the armed-troop,

A narchy abounds as The Eleven break free,

I nto darkness they've fled, but The Man does not flee.

N or has the one-Damned sought to hide or escape,

S till standing unveiled as the moon is cloud-draped -

T hese Two have their eyes on the story they'll shape.

---

13 **MAT 26:48-49; MRK 14:44-45; LUK 22:47-48.**

SCENE 2: Annas' house.
(With elders, scribes, servants, etc.)

T he descent into Judgement has gone as designed,

H enceforth will this drama keep Scriptural-Time:

E vents have been pre-set to the hours assigned...

M aking their way through the dense metropole,

A nnas' house is partly-lit and patrolled; [14]

N ow the ones in attendance are of the same fold. [15]

T he detail arrives while the city still sleeps,

H urried and jostled is The Man in their keep,

A Disciple attends; (who first came in the night):

T was Cephas who stirred him soon after his flight.

I nside, The Disciple, soon uncovers the facts,

S tating concerns against this clandestine act.

M oving past servants; he finds the Accused,

Y et he fears that this crisis can not be diffused.

---

14 **JHN 18:13.**
15 **The Sadducean Priesthood / Pharisaic leaders.**

F or The Man is confuting their charges as lies;

E nraging them all, til The Disciple advised:

L et the Feast-Days be kept and this matter delayed,

L est we profane what our Fathers ordained and obeyed! –

O n that motion they vote; (but to elsewhere convene),

W ith a wave of his hand, Annas switches the scene.

SCENE 3: Outside Caiaphas house.
(With guards, servants, etc.)

S ome guards warm their hands from a glowing coal-fire [16]

M arking the time til they're relieved or retired. –

I nto this courtyard, The Disciple has come:

T he decision 'twas routed - to Caiaphas, his son; [17]

E yeing the grounds, he looks desperate and glum.

T he rendezvous with Cephas takes place unobserved,

H idden from view; (round a pillar he's curved),

E xposing himself, he seems tense and disturbed.

The Disciple - Simon Peter:

S haped were their minds ere this travesty began,

H elped by Iscariot who furthered their plans.

E rratic, mixed-sources have been coached or coerced;

P ressured were elders with censure or worse.

Glancing around.

H ereupon his face stiffens as the council's espied,

E xtending his hand, into the palace he strides.

R esuming his place, Peter's nerve starts to fail,

D istracted in thought, he's soon spotted and hailed:

A rt thou not a disciple of The Prisoner detained?:

N o one here can vouchsafe your odd-presence or name –

D eny thou wast captured when Malchus was maimed?... [18]

---

16 **MRK 14:54, LUK 22:55.**
17 **MAT 26:57.**
18 **JHN 18:10.**

T hese questions all weaken his composure and heart:

H is stealth is uncovered; they've remembered his part,

E vading their eyes, he thrice denies and departs.

S eeking swift-safety, and Solitude's self-state,

H is words hounds his steps as he hurries his gait,

E ventually he slows; and near a wall high and steep,

E arly movements are heard as the rising-sun creeps –

P eter halts when the cock crows - and remembering, weeps.

SCENE 4: Inside Caiaphas house.
(With guards, servants, etc.)

Caiaphas - The Disciple:

S pake he not of a Kingdom which would all kingdoms rend,

H ath his purse-keep not said he must die for this end? -

A s for the Powers-that-be; he's our bait and their snare,

L et him die for the people, and if this Nation be spared, [19]

L et the lost-Tribes re-gather under our priestly care.

Caiaphas - The Captain of the Guards:

B ind him with tethers, and with the rays of first light,

E x-tra-dite him to Pilate - he will heed common plight.

Caiaphas(Aside) – JESUS:

S o many messiahs have vainly promised and failed;

C an a blaspheming-bastard be the one who prevails? –

A s for those of your cult and that Lazarus trick; [20]

T his day shall disprove what they believe and predict.

JESUS – Caiaphas:

T his Day was approved, and ere your Council adjourns,

E ven know you've fulfilled what you've meant to o'erturn -

R e-cycled is Time - for ***This Day*** circles round, [21]

E 'en then shall you see me with bent-knee, and head-down,

D escending in triumph with Heaven's High-Crowns.

Exeunt all.

---

19 **JHN 11:47-53; JHN 18:14.**
20 **JHN 11:1-46; JHN 12:1-11.**
21 **ZEC 12:10; MAT 26:64; MRK 14:62; LUK 22:69; REV 19:11-16.**
The dynamics surrounding this Passover will be discussed in a future work.
AUTHOR.

ENTR'ACTE

Legio(Chanting).

K ill the twin-scapegoat, and pollute the cursed-tree,[22]

A zazel must die, so let this other go free,

R eject his Blood-Smear, and this epitaph append:

A ngelic-defiance shall all Prophecy suspend.

T hen shall That Woman abort her own Seed, [23]

H eralding an end to what the Garden decreed.

---

22 This is the First Entr'acte Acrostic: **KARATH:** 3772 karath kaw-rath' a primitive root; to cut (off, down or asunder); by implication, to destroy or consume; specifically, to covenant(i.e. make an alliance or bargain, originally by cutting flesh and passing between the pieces):--be chewed, be con-(feder-) ate, covenant,cut (down, off), destroy, fail, feller, be freed, hew (down), make a league ((covenant)), X lose, perish, X utterly, X want. **STRONG'S CONCORDANCE.**
23 **GEN 3:14-15.**

ACT II
SCENE 1: Pilate's bedroom.

I mages kept streaming through her half-conscious state, [24]

H astening figures who seem hurried or late.

A brupt are their movements, and rude are their tongues,

V exed is their manner; their tempers high-strung,

E xcitement is mounting over what has begun.

S wept up in the rush, she is caught and embraced,

U ntil the dream changes scenes and elsewhere she's placed;

F amiliar one site; but by Jewry decried,

F ixed 'gainst the stone-walls, is **The Fortress** espied: [25]

E nclosed and surveilling, toward the sky it is reared,

R esting next Herod's temple, it is hated and feared. -

E ast of this vantage, Olive's top is aglow:

D awn's rays yawn like arms to the cocks-waking crow.

M urmurring shadows switch the vision-perceived,

A s **Antonia** bestirs, and the watch is relieved: -

N orth-east of the Palace, a thin-column is gleaned; [26]

Y oked is a yeanling; yea, yielding and yeaned.

---

24 This is the Third Acrostic: **I have suffered many things this day in a dream because of him** - MAT **27:19.**
25 **Antonia.**
26 **Herod's Palace.**

T he Man in her focus is pushed through the streets,

H is features are blurry; and his captors' discreet.

I n seconds they near the Prefectures gate,

N ew voices are heard, and they're ordered to wait.

G oading forth The One held, they his seditions enlarge,

S teeled are their eyes when the guards hear the charge.

T hence a marching of footsteps, well-quickened and sure,

H er husband is wakened; they've arrived at the door.

I n her bed, still asleep, she bares witness to all -

S he endeavors to rise, but into slumber she falls.

D rawn up through the clouds, to a temple she's shown,

A Pantheon stands there, bowing low to one throne –

Y ea, her gods aren't chiseled any longer in stone.

I ntense is their silence til the one they all dread

N ext turns his blank eyes to this dreamer instead,

A nd in faraway tones moves this message ahead:

Satan(As King of the Gods):

D espair not of this place, nor our persons intent,

R equired of thee is but thy free will consent.

E re the Future becomes, we may its course sometimes steer;

A s for that vow you once made for thy spouses career

M ay by us be approved, if thy heart proves sincere.

Pointing around,

B y these gods ye are praised; (who rule Mortal-kind),

E ven so I must know where your motives incline.

C hanges bring fortunes to the favorites we know

A nd on such may we gods these great fortunes bestow. -

U nderway is a plan that will raise rebel aims;

S hewn in thy vision is The One they will frame;

E vents will turn badly if he's sum-mar-i-ly blamed.

Pausing,

O ut of hate they've ensnared him, to spare their own seed, [27]

F or the one they'll prefer will wage wars to be freed...

H ave faith in us gods - and let That Man be redeemed,

I n pursuance thereof we shall thy husband esteem –

M ount Olympus awaits - and the **Sanhedrin** schemes.

---

27 **MAT 27:18, MRK 15:10.**

SCENE 2: Pilate's hall.
(With officers, guards, servants, etc.)

P ower was wielded by this governor's un-skilled, [28]

I nflexible, vindictive, and relentless self-will.

L oathing the people, his office, and place,

A series of sleights would he inflict on that race: -

T iberian-ensigns first provoked holy zeal [29]

E nraging the city until removed by appeal.

A fter this, gilded-shields, would profane Herod's palace, [30]

S training relations with calculating malice. -

K orban also was spent; and an aquaduct installed, [31]

E xciting the Jews who were piqued and appalled;

D eterrence came swift, with scores murdered or mauled.

---

28 This is the Fourth Acrostic: **(Pilate) asked whether the man were a Galilaean - LUK 23:6.**
...for he(Pilate) was a man of a very inflexible disposition, and very merciless as well as very obstinate, ...in respect of his corruption, and his acts of insolence, and his rapine, and his habit of insulting people, and his cruelty, and his continual murders of people untried and uncondemned, and his never ending, and gratuitous, and most grievous inhumanity. **PHILO - On The Embassy of Gauis Book XXXVIII 299-305.**
29 Now Pilate, who was sent as procurator into Judea by Tiberius, sent by night those **images of Caesar** that are called ensigns into Jerusalem. This excited a very great tumult among the Jews when it was day;...
On the next day Pilate sat upon his tribunal, in the open market-place, and called to him the multitude,...
Hereupon Pilate was greatly surprised at their prodigious superstition, and gave order that the ensigns should be presently carried out of Jerusalem. **JOSEPHUS - WARS.2.9.2-3.**
30 He(PILATE), not more with the object of doing honour to Tiberius than with that of vexing the multitude, dedicated some **gilt shields** in the palace of Herod, in the holy city;... **PHILO - On The Embassy of Gauis Book XXXVIII 299 -305.**
31 After this he(Pilate) raised another disturbance, by expending that sacred treasure which is called **Corban** upon aqueducts, whereby he brought water from the distance of four hundred furlongs. At this the multitude had indignation; and when Pilate was come to Jerusalem, they came about his tribunal, and made a clamor at it. Now when he was apprized aforehand of this disturbance, he mixed his own soldiers in their armor with the multitude, and ordered them to conceal themselves under the habits of private men, and not indeed to use their swords, but with their staves to beat those that made the clamor. He then gave the signal from his tribunal [to do as he had bidden them]. Now the Jews were so sadly beaten, that many of them perished by the stripes they received, and many of them perished as trodden to death by themselves; by which means the multitude was astonished at the calamity of those that were slain, and held their peace. **JOSEPHUS - WARS.2.9.4.175-177.**
But Pilate undertook to bring a current of water to Jerusalem, and did it with the **sacred money,** and derived the origin of the stream from the distance of two hundred furlongs. However, the Jews were not pleased with what had been done about this water; and many ten thousands of the people got together, and made a clamor against him, and insisted that he should leave off that design. Some of them also used reproaches, and abused the man, as crowds of such people usually do. So he habited a great number of his soldiers in their habit, who carried daggers under

W ith each vicious act would he fuel discontent;

H arassment and insults would be met with dissent.

E xchanges were common, and ere the Province would rend,

T erse letters of outrage to the Emperor were penned.[32]

H earing their plaint, and this threat to World-Peace,

E mphatically he ordered this injustice to cease –

R ealizing his plight, Pilate tempered his reach.

T o this mis-an-thrope's hall, was Our Shepherd conveyed,

H is captors hoped matters might be speedily weighed,

E xpecting their Pasch might be stopped or delayed.

M easuring his patience, the Prefect advised:

A lthough my appointment's been challenged and sized,

N o urgings or threats will my oath compromise.

W ith feigning respect, they assuage his complaint,

E vincing their fealty and their civil-restraint;

R ehearsed and trite-phrased, and from memory-inscribed,

E ach one turns his focus on The Man to be tried

---

their garments, and sent them to a place where they might surround them. So he bid the Jews himself go away; but they boldly casting reproaches upon him, he gave the soldiers that signal which had been beforehand agreed on; who laid upon them much greater blows than Pilate had commanded them, and equally punished those that were tumultuous, and those that were not; nor did they spare them in the least: and since the people were unarmed, and were caught by men prepared for what they were about, there were a great number of them slain by this means, and others of them ran away wounded. And thus an end was put to this sedition. **JOSEPHUS - ANTIQ.18.3.2.60-62.**
32 And those who were in power in our nation, seeing this, and perceiving that he was inclined to change his mind as to what he had done, but that he was not willing to be thought to do so, wrote a most supplicatory letter to Tiberius. **PHILO - On The Embassy of Gauis Book XXXVIII 299- 305.**

Enter a Messenger.

As a note's passed to Pilate to beware this month's Ides. [33]

Gaunt-rimmed were his eyes as he looked up from the text,

Alarming the party this may their purpose deflect.

Lacking a spokesman, they in concert re-warn:

In Galilee's hills; where Rome's rebels are spawned,

Lives he, The Accused, in that bed of unrest,

And our Council believes a quick judgement is best.

Pilate(stalling for time) then,

Even so it should be, but by me it won't come,

As he is Galilaean, ye must seek Herod's third son [34]

Now deliver him henceforth, for this hearing is done.

Exeunt all.

---

33 Passover Day occurs on the the 15th day of Nisan. **AUTHOR.**

34 **Herod Antipas.**
When Caesar had heard these pleadings, he dissolved the assembly; but a few days afterwards he appointed **(1)** - **ARCHELAUS,** not indeed to be king of the whole country, but ethnarch of the one half of that which had been subject to Herod, and promised to give him the royal dignity hereafter, if he governed his part virtuously. But as for the other half, he divided it into two parts, and gave it to two other of Herod's sons, to **(2) - PHILIP** and to **(3) - ANTIPAS,** that Antipas who disputed with Archelaus for the whole kingdom. Now to him it was that Peres and Galilee paid their tribute, which amounted annually to two hundred talents, while Batanea, with Trachonitis, as well as Auranitis, with a certain part of what was called the *House of Lenodorus,* paid the tribute of one hundred talents to Philip; but Idumea, and Judea, and the country of Samaria paid tribute to Archelaus, but had now a fourth part of that tribute taken off by the order of Caesar, who decreed them that mitigation, because they did not join in this revolt with the rest of the multitude. There were also certain of the cities which paid tribute to Archelaus: Strato's Tower and Sebaste, with Joppa and Jerusalem; for as to Gaza, and Gadara, and Hippos, they were Grecian cities, which Caesar separated from his government, and added them to the province of Syria. Now the tribute-money that came to Archelaus every year from his own dominions amounted to six hundred talents. **ANTIQ.17.11.4.317-320.**

ENTR'ACTE
Legio(Chanting).

G ather light-hearted spells and debase royal tongues, [35]

A ffect a mood-swing, and let their cares be unstrung.

D isarm and deceive Edom's-King with dark-charms,

A nd laugh that bound-fool back to Pilates strict-arm.

---

35 This is the Second Entr 'acte Acrostic: **GADA**: 1438 gada 'gaw-dah' a primitive root; to fell a tree; generally, to destroy anything:--cut (asunder, in sunder, down, off),hew down. **STRONG 'S CONCORDANCE.**

ACT III
SCENE 1: Herod's bedroom.

A ntipas had wakened to his moaning wife's pain, [36]

N ight-terrors had plagued her since The Baptist was slain:

D epression's dark drug was dosed daily and drained.

H erod himself often brooded and sighed,

E xpecting some respite was at last drawing nigh.

R omancing rife-rumors regarding Re-birth;

O n hearing The Man was some Prophet of worth, [37]

D eluded himself that John now stalked the Earth.

S o dwelt his dementia when the sentries drew near,

A nnouncing a party had abruptly appeared;

I n haste he assembled and ordered his train,

D etermined this intrusion be quickly explained.

---

36 This is the Fifth Acrostic: **(And Herod said), This is John the Baptist; he is risen from the dead - MAT 14:2.
Herodias.**
MAT 14:3; MRK 6:19; LUK 3:19-20.
37 **MAT 14:1-2; MRK 6:14-16.**

SCENE 2: Herods throne room.
(With guards, servants, etc.)

T he elders related how the matter evolved;

H ow the Prefect preferred he this case should resolve.

I nfused with elation by this sign of respect, [38]

S mugly he signals to summon in the suspect.

I nstantly The Man is thrust into his den –

S eizing the moment, The Fox slyly contends: [39]

Herod – JESUS:

J ustice-blindfolded has both fore- and hind-sight:

O uter vision oft clouds first-perception with Right.

H ence may my record; (dated as it was learned),

N egate these grave charges or their verity affirm.

Pausing,

T hy converts were noted, and thy footsteps pursued,

H idden in crowds; spies reported the mood;

E ach Sermon was ciphered - each Miracle reviewed.

B etween Roman Law and the Jewish Tradition,

A droitly you trode, leaving only suspicion.

P easant-protected on every road and detour,

T able and lodging came from a welcoming door.

I n Galilee, Samaria, Sidon, and Tyre,

S undry attested that thy works were inspired -

(Leaning forward,)

38 **LUK 23:8-12.**
39 **LUK 13:31-32.**

T he High-Priest is sure that your mission conspired.

H appily, perhaps, this was all happenstance,

E xtend me thy version and give Justice a chance.

Enter Herodias with attendants.

I n the waiting that followed, his incestuous-bride,

S urveying the scene, swiftly strode to his side.

R estive she sat, then in a voice strained and tense:

I s John-Redivivus come seeking his vengeance?

Caiaphas' party(In the background).

S uspecting her mood would affect the Court-Royal,

E fforts began to divert her turmoil-

N ew rumors were proffered that he sought the King's-Spoils.

An Elder to Antipas:

F rom the first he called David both his father and son [40]

R evealing his birth solved that Psalm's conundrum.

O n other occasions, our operatives observed;

M ention was made at GOD'S right hand he served...

Sustained silence.

T he laughter first started when Herodias bowed down,

H erod, on cue, lent his robe-Purple and Crown.

E ach one, in their turn, aped the mirth of a clown.

D elirium gave way to face-slaps and hate-spit;

E ntertainment-noir for The Man in the midst.

---

40 **PSA 2:7; PSA 110; MAT 22:41-46; MRK 12:35-37; LUK 20:41-44.**

A s the morning aged on, one thing became sure –

D estiny would knock twice on Pilate's front door.

Exeunt all.

ENTR'ACTE
Legio(Chanting).

G uiding his life by the lines in his hand,[41]

A ntipas was **CUT** from the script that we planned. –

Z ion's gate has been breached; we can settle therein:

A ligned with our Prefect, he'll oppose his own kin [42]

R eady the next phase - Pilate's role soon begins.

---

41 This is the Third Entr'acte Acrostic: **GAZAR:** 1504 gazar gaw-zar' a primitive root; to cut down or off; (figuratively) to destroy, divide, exclude, or decide:-- cut down (off), decree, divide, snatch. **STRONG'S CONCORDANCE**.

42 **LUK 23:12.**
N.B.1 - Since Idumea(Edom) was first forced into Judaism by John Hyrcanus of the Hasmonean Dynasty in the 2nd Century B.C.(**JOSEPHUS - ANTIQ.13.9.1.257-258**), Herod Antipas, like his father before him(Herod the Great), had sought acceptance and legitimacy from the Jewish Religious Authority(s) / Population.
N.B.2 - Pilate had also offended Jewish sensitivities because of his intractable nature. **SEE ACT II, SCENE 2 FOOTNOTES 28-32.**
N.B.3 - The Sadducean Priesthood, as well as the leading Pharisees, were determined that after the Lazarus incident(**JHN 11:47-54; 18:14**), that he, JESUS, as well as Lazarus(**JHN 12:10-11**), should be put to death for the nation.
N.B.4 - With Herod now friends with Pilate and both **CUT OFF** from the same Religious Authority(s); the probability of a JESUS conviction, now officially unsupported by both Herod's and Pilate's lenient treatment of the charges, would have seemed to have become diminished.
N.B.5 - The Satanically-placed figure of Bar-abbas, which would now enter the scene, was meant to **ensure** a JESUS release. Bar-abbas, as well as other Jewish rebels, had always offered the possibility that a Deliverer might one day appear to free the people from the Roman Empire. It was this Bar-abbas factor and image, that the Satanic influence hoped would overturn a JESUS conviction and Passover by offering a Messiah-like substitute for the **ISA 53:8** and **DAN 9:26a** Prophecy(s). A Bar-abbas conviction would have **fulfilled** the superficial requirement of a Messiah who was **CUT OFF**, but it would have also **unfulfilled** the Spiritual Promise - by **CUTTING OFF** the real purpose behind those twin Prophecy(s).
N.B.6 - Within this Supernatural/Political framework, the Satanic influence(**DAN 7:25c**) over its FOURTH KINGDOM ROMAN EMPIRE **was** able to foil any joint Herodian and Sadducean support for a Bar-Abbas release, thus advancing the possibility of **derailing** the JESUS-Passover. It could not however, negate the **ISA 53:8** and **DAN 9:26a** Prophecy(s), which stated that he, JESUS, a Priest after the Order of Melchizedek(**PSA 110:4; HEB 5-7**) would be **CUT OFF** by his own people, i.e., the Sadducean priesthood, the Pharisaic leaders, and their closest followers. It should be noted that the multitudes, when not intimidated by these Religious Leaders, had welcomed JESUS into Jerusalem – **MAT 21:1-17; MRK 11:1-11; LUK 19:29-40; JHN 12:12-19.**
N.B.7 - Finally, all Divine Prophecy takes place within the irreversible Will of the **MOST-HIGH**; and whatever reactions it will create during it's execution, both Free-will and Demonic-will are eventually confounded in it's fulfillment - **JOB 5:13.**
AUTHOR.

ACT IV
SCENE 1: Pilate chamber's.

H is brow shadowed worry, and his mood was disturbed, [43]

A waiting his wife, he re-examined her words:

V isions from god! - Pray spare the defendant!

E xonerate The Man! - Note the date is impendent!...

T he thrust of the message, and the directive it bade,

H ad entered his Court as an obstruction well-played.

O nly luck and legality had changed the venue,

U nnerved at its timing, he the contents reviewed.

Pilates wife arrives.

N o greeting was offered when she entered the room;

O n news of The Man; she feared their Future was doomed.

T he die had been cast – but then a soldier reports:

H erod likewise defers, and yields The Man to your Court.

I n the moments thereaft; they a fresh outlook convey,

N oting the celebrants who had come for this day,

G azing out at the city - her fears are allayed.

T oward the west the Moon sets as the eastern Sun Climbs

O 'er the menacing Tower, looming fierce and sublime.

D esiring the shade his wife shuns the packed street –

O n her heels The Man lags in the glare of its heat.

---

43 This is the Sixth Acrostic: **Have thou nothing to do with that just man - MAT 27:19.**

SCENE 2: Pilate's hall.
(With officers, guards, servants, etc.)

**Enter Caiaphas' party,
sent back by Herod Antipas.**

W ary of time, an Elder bluntly asserts:

I ncitement to riot grows with his every convert.

T roubling the Peace, on an ass he hath ridden,

H ailed about as The King who'd make tribute forbidden. [44]

T his last allegation placed The Man against Rome,

H ereafter must Pilate as the Prefect be known;

A ssessing the crowd, which has grown since the Hour;

T his case seems bewitched by some Genii-empowered.

Pilate(worried) – JESUS:

J ustice they'll howl, but I know their base heart,

U nless thou contest, I must swift Judgement impart.

JESUS(calmly) – Pilate:

S hall the captor play captive to his captives thereof?

T hou couldest no Power have, except that from above. - [45]

M istaking these words have confirmed his wife's vision,

A ssured is he henceforth of his course and decision -

N ow the choice shall be left to a rootless tradition. [46]

Exeunt all.

---

44 **MAT 22:21, MRK 12:17, LUK 20:25.**
45 **JHN 19:11.**
46 **MAT 27:15; MRK 15:6; LUK 23:17; JHN 18:39.**

ENTR'ACTE
Legio(Chanting).

K indle mad-hate toward every rebel enchained,[47]

A nnas' son may not such outrage contain.

R esolved is our will, we've devised an outcome;

A fter all preparations, this matter's fore-done.

T oday we shall reckon sweet-closure for all;

H owl into the crowd and outshout these paid-Thralls. [48]

---

47 This is the Fourth Entr'acte Acrostic: **KARATH:** 3772 karath kaw-rath' a primitive root; to cut (off, down or asunder); by implication, to destroy or consume; specifically, to covenant(i.e. make an alliance or bargain, originally by cutting flesh and passing between the pieces):--be chewed, be con-(feder-) ate, covenant,cut (down, off), destroy, fail, feller, be freed, hew (down), make a league ((covenant)), X lose, perish, X utterly, X want. **STRONG'S CONCORDANCE.**
48 **MAT 27:20; MRK 15:11; LUK 23:23.**

ACT V
SCENE 1: Outside The Pavement(Gabbatha).
(Massing crowd of guards, elders, scribes, servants, officers, soldiers, etc.)

A lerted by servants how the affair had progressed, [49]

N oting the lateness, and the thickening-press;

D read and excitement beat within Caiaphas' breast.

F ew blocked his passage as he pushed through the mix,

R ousing his jurors to beware Pilate's tricks.

O n this day, at **The Pavement,** soldiers-armed are deployed; [50]

M onitors and spies are in their functions employed.

---

49 This is the Seventh Acrostic: **And from thenceforth Pilate sought to release him - JHN 19:12.**
50 **JHN 19:13.**

SCENE 2: Pilate's chambers.

T he tension has mounted, like the mid-morning Sun,

H eating crowd-madness, who for the Custom had come.

E motions, long-pent, may in this hour erupt,

N earing a frenzy which might be hard to disrupt.

C ombing the crowd Pilate's men have comprised

E vidence that rebels might be armed and disguised.

F aced with the prospect of sudden riot or worse,

O rders are pending to promptly rout and disperse.

R esolved in his purpose, Pilate suddenly appears,

T umultuous loud-screams box and deafen his ears -

H isteria subsides into half-hearted jeers.

SCENE 3: Outside The Pavement(Gabbatha).

Pilate, before the crowd:

P oised and remote, he then makes this address:

I n deference to peace does Caesar grant one request:[51]

L et all present here, who for Justice have come,

A dhere to this Custom where a wrong is undone.

Pausing,

T his day I've a man in whom no guilt has been found.

E xamined by scourging; his character proved sound.

S ignalling his guards, they The Man now expose,

Enter JESUS the CHRIST.

O utfitted in purple which Antipas had chose.

U nbandaged fresh-wounds stained the mant'let dark-red;

G hostly-pale is the image over which that robe spreads.

H aphazardly set is a mixed-tangle of thorns:

T ight-laced and well-platted in a headdress of scorn.

T aunts are soon heard; from every corner they rise,

O f Bar-Abbas they roar in their repeated outcries: [52]

---

51 MAT 27:15; MRK 15:6; LUK 23:17; JHN 18:39.
52 MAT 27:20-26; MRK 15:11-15; LUK 23:18-25; JHN 19:6,15.

Enter Jesus Bar-Abbas.
The crowd points to JESUS the CHRIST.

R evealed is *thy* choice, but your scourging has lied,

E xclaimed more than once, 'He sits at GOD'S right hand side. [53]

L et Bar-Abbas go free; he's no god, but a man,

E xcept he's released, Caesar's rival's at hand.

A nath-ema is he to your Roman design,

S o too does this Bastard taint our future and kind;

E xonerate Bar-Abbas, we are all of one mind.

The crowd continues to shout for Jesus Bar-Abbas.

H alf-stunned and unnerved, Pilate yields and retreats,

I n his wandering mind he knows the gods have been beat -

M aking towards a near basin, he reflects on defeat.

Exeunt all save Pilate,
who is still washing his hands.

ENTR'ACTE
Satan – Legio:

G et the Legions en route, for our effort's been checked,[54]

A dvance their positions and prepare for what's next.

D amnation is certain if we accept this setback,

A ll is not lost if we change not from our tack!

---

53 **PSA 110; MAT 26:64; MRK 14:62; LUK 22:69.**
54   This is the Fifth Entr 'acte Acrostic: **GADA**: 1438 gada 'gaw-dah' a primitive root; to fell a tree; generally, to destroy anything:--cut (asunder, in sunder, down, off),hew down. **STRONG 'S CONCORDANCE.**

EPILOGUE

T he gavel of auction and judgement descends, [55]

H alting the sun near it's first-quarter's end. [56]

E ventually the search for the sound and it's source

W earied the eye til Nature resumed it's old course.

A s with each of their Feasts, all was rote and routine;

G uests would arrive; there'd be nothing foreseen,

E xpectations were there, but for another man's day,

S ave for Three who were damned for the roles they had played...

O f the Jesus released, he would seek Modern-shores [57]

F athering a Clan which would oppose Christian-mores.

S econd to follow, without conscience or friend; [58]

---

55 This is the Eighth Acrostic: **The wages of sin is death - ROM 6:23.**

56 **The Four Quarters of the Day.**

N.B.1 - 0600 - 0900(Third Hour) is the 1st quarter - BEGINNING OF CRUCIFIXION(Third Hour).
   MRK 15:25.

N.B.2 - 0900 - 1200(Sixth Hour) is the 2nd quarter - BEGINNING OF THREE HOURS OF DARKNESS(Sixth Hour).
   MAT 27:45; MRK 15:33; LUK 23:44.

N.B.3 - **JHN 19:14** is inconsistent with the above accounts.

N.B.4 - 1200 - 1500(Ninth Hour) is the 3rd quarter - DEATH OF JESUS, TEMPLE VEIL RENT, THE EARTH QUAKES, SAINTS RESURRECT(Ninth Hour).
   MAT 27:46-53; MRK 15:34-38; LUK 23:45-46; JHN 19:30.

N.B.5 - 1500 - 1800(Twelfth Hour) is the 4th quarter – JOSEPH OF ARIMATHAEA & NICODEMUS RETRIEVE BODY OF JESUS, JESUS PLACED IN SEPULCHRE(B4 Sundown – Twelfth Hour), BEGINNING OF PASSOVER(Twelfth Hour?).
   MAT 27:54-61; MRK 15:39-47; LUK 23:47-56; JHN 19:31-42.

AUTHOR.

57 **Jesus Bar-Abbas.**

N.B.1 - 912.Barabbas bar-ab-bas of Chaldee origin ((1347 and 5); son of Abba; Bar-abbas,an Israelite:--Barabbas.
STRONG 'S CONCORDANCE.

N.B.2 – Barabbas' name appears as **bar-Abbas** in the Greek texts. It is derived ultimately from the Aramaic, **Bar-abba**, 'son of the father'. According to early Greek texts, Barabbas' full name was **Jesus Barabbas.** Later texts shorten his name to just **Barabbas. WIKIPEDIA.**

58 **ACT 1:15-19.**

I mpelled by cruel-vipers to seek his land's end.

N agged by their voices to A-cel-dam-a's blood-field,

I mmolation was wrought on a tree without yield.

S o ends their Two parts - but of those not yet slain,

D eath would now drag to the place long-ordained…

E ach one bore the crossbeam upon which he must die,

A nd as Golgotha's stone-eyes saw their sentence applied, [59]

T he bleating of sheep in the background was heard;

H asting observance from the Pasch-unobserved.

ENTR'ACTE
Satan(Soliloquy):

G ehenna now pulls; (and in its throes shall they sink), [60]

A bducting them all to the bottomless brink –

Satan(Half-raging):

Z ealots and hirelings have up-turned my Time-table,

A nd ruined the plan which would have furthered their Fable. -

R everse will I this, and this Prophecy disable.

Exeunt.

---

59 **MAT 27:33; MRK 15:22; JHN 19:17.**
60 This is the Sixth Entr'acte Acrostic: **GAZAR:** 1504 gazar gaw-zar' a primitive root; to cut down or off; (figuratively) to destroy, divide, exclude, or decide:-- cut down (off), decree, divide, snatch. **STRONG'S CONCORDANCE.**

THE CRUCIFIXION

DRAMATIS PERSONAE

JESUS, the Son of GOD.

The Thieves   } Dimas,

   } Gestas.

Satan, as the Image-Grotesque & Angel of Light.

The Women   } Mary, the mother of JESUS,

   } Mary Magdalene,

   } Mary, the wife of Cleophas.

The Beloved Disciple.

The Avenger or Angel of Death.

Guards, Bystanders, Legions of Hell, etc.

THE SCENE: Golgotha.

PART I

Now Gibeon's mid-Sun is occulted on high, [1]

As day becomes night to the witnessing eye;

And Ajalon's full-Moon keeps her aspect opposed,

Underfoot of The Women bewailing their woes.

Before the skull's face loom three crosses upright, [2]

Aflamed in an aura of unnatural light;

As a low-moaning wind swirls about the grim scene;

Anxiety mounts and pervades the crowd's being.

The guards crouch about in superstition and dread,

As the low-moaning wind channels cries from the dead;

In lingering whispers and dire rumors they warn,

That payment will follow the man that is scorned.

As the bystanders point and GOD'S judgement assign,

The Thieves fling back insults when these hecklers malign;

But The Third in his agony - wracked in body and soul,

Notes in horror how Death is exacting what's scrolled:

---

1 **JOS 10:12.**
2 **MAT 27:33; MRK 15:22; JHN 19:17.**

Let his strength be a potsherd, dry-weathered and flawed, [3]

Let his tongue swell from thirst within slackening jaws.

Let him pour out like water, let his bones be disjoined,

Let fear rend his Soul from his heart through his groin.

Let the dogs snarl about, let the wicked enclose,

Let his hands be nail-pierced, and his person exposed.

Let him see all his bones; let him count every one,

Let his garments and vesture be wagered and won.

With each labored breath would the same chant revive,

And with each iteration would his sanity strive;

Over and over would it sear and engrave

On his Soul as it slipped ever nearer the Grave.

Twas 'bout the Sixth hour when their bodies slumped down, [4]

As the Void slowly oped into which they were bound;

Into there they descended; (states the Psalmist in Time), [5]

Each branded or traded for Bar-Abbas' crime.

It was here in this Void 'twixt the Quick and the Dead,

That their last dying words before the Damned would be said.

It was here where this Drama never written unfolds,

And it is here where the Truth of this story is told.

---

3 **PSA 22:14-18.**
4 **MAT 27:45-46; MRK 15:33-34; LUK 23:44.**
5 **PSA 16:10; ACT 2:31.**

Overwhelmed and exhausted; pulled by Death's undertow,

In unconscious pain, toward that empty below,

Their minds drift and wander, and by delusions are swayed,

As a nightmarish gathering out of nowhere has strayed.

From anear and afar, toward this Bottomless world,

Massed hunched-crook'ed forms and bent vulture-like churls;

Mixed-hybrids and mutants of gross image and kind,

Who un-bred their first likeness to erase GOD'S-design.

Herein marched the Star-thrones; (past Lord's of Creation),

Who plotted since Eden to regain their lost stations.

For vengeance they came; for this day was appointed,

To mark the blood-rite that would kill The Anointed.

O 'ersoaring the deep screeched a Cockatrice red-grey,

With wide-spanning wings and whipping tailbone in play

Chain-plated and layered; (like articulated mail),

Of its Genus and Species: 'twas without Natures scale.

As the Three forms be-stir, and the dark Ether splits,

Two gape in full-horror as their sense of where shifts,

Toward The One in the midst flies that menacing Foe,

Who now orders Pale-Death to withhold its last blow.

Before The Man-helpless, he hovers in place,

Afloat in the airless, breathless vacuum of space;

On effortless beats of his wings is he perched,

As he pronounces a tongue never uttered on Earth:

PART II

Satan(as Image-Grotesque) – JESUS:

A wake! and behold!, and discern this lost place; [6]

N ote the kindred you've spurned now observes your disgrace, -

D eath's hand shall be stayed till my judgement is faced.

Addressing his Legions:

A ll ye Light-Beings of dawn and our Great Enterpise;

F aithful warriors who thwart what *his* GOD would devise,

T his hour fulfills what we willed would be slated:

E xploit or expel whom the Timeline awaited -

R egarding Bar-Abbas - his life is still fated.

Pointing to JESUS,

T hat false-GOD'S Messiah barely clings to his life,

H is mission's aborted without protest or strife.

R endezvous and rencounter - yea, the battle was won,

E re the male Royal-Heir could become *that* GOD'S Son.

E xamine the past; - before the Scepter divided: [7]

S tone idols and worship were the means that provided

C orrective reproof, which disjointed the Nation,

O rdering the split that enforced separation. - [8]

R ent was their Kingdom when we cut That King's line; [9]

E masculating his throne and its Heirs for all time.

---

6 This is the First Acrostic: **And after threesore and two weeks shall Messiah be CUT OFF, but not for himself -
DAN 9:26.**
7 **1 KNGS 12:20.**
8 **1 KNGS 11:9-13; 1 KNGS 12:21-24; 2 CHR 10; 2 CHR 11:1-4.**
9 **Solomon.**

Addressing his Right Wing:

A dvance and stand ready, lest *his* GOD 'tempt some feat.

N egation of Prophecy must provoke his conceit. -

D oomsday's Clock will re-set with this Lamb's final bleat.

Giving a hand signal:

T wo squadrons aloft! - and patrol this Star's edge,

W atch for signs of *his* GOD to regain his failed-pledge,

O ur doorway won't close if *his* Messiah's in-wedged. –

Addressing his Legions:

W eary not of the conflict, for our goals are at hand,

E very venture well-played disrupts his laid plan.

E xamine our prey - this is *he* who was vaunted,

K ept hidden since birth till the day *he* was flaunted-

S hall Star-Beings immortal by mortals be daunted?

S hall Nobility-Ordained be robbed of their place,

H arassed by some deity who o'erlords his own race? -

A ll creatures are fashioned - and by Nature's design,

L eaving rule to the fittest - not by *his* GOD assigned.

Pointing to JESUS,

L o, *This Word* was *his* tenure which we've undermined.

His followers begin to jeer.

M yriads uncounted, let not his wrong's be inflated,

E numerate them not - let all in one be conflated.

S uffice it to say, that to uplift the clay-forms,

S ubvert the Angelics - he'd exalt the Mud-born. -

I n spite of their patterns of lower behavior

A nd futile attempts by religious soothsayers,

H e preached and pretended to be their Lord-Savior.

Rising laughter.
Satan(as Image-Grotesque) – JESUS:

B y your own law be judged; which *your* GOD can't amend,

E xpect the same mercy which a dissembler condemns:

C an Spirits cross-dress, and be not what they wear?

U n-spin thy clay-garment and reveal what is there. -

Scornfully:

T hy pottery of flesh is but i-dol-a-trous wear!

Exulting:

O nan was his Sire, and Lilith his Wet-Nurse: [10]

F oster Father and Mother to a Child-accursed.

F oundling or not - thou art a Mamzer and worse! [11]

More laughter and jeering.

---

10 **GEN 38:1-10.**
11 **Bastard.** 4464 mamzer mam-zare' from an unused root meaning to alienate; a mongrel, i.e. born of a Jewish father and a heathen mother:--bastard. **STRONG'S CONCORDANCE.**

These vaunts break like thunder rolling off a war- drum,

And like a sheep to be sheared he seems helpless and dumb.

But this tirade must rage till his last breath of life,

When the cursed Beast of Eden provokes his own strife.

PART III

The Thieves are unnerved by the commotion un-leashed,[12]

And their fears are compounded for they ken not his speech.

As the howling subsides, The Beast eyes the said two,

And with unswerving aim his agenda pursues.

Wafting slowly around he floats clear out of sight,

Beyond the spent-forms; in this Netherworld's light,

There he sheds his first form and into another he goes,

And from behind The Three crosses an identity grows.

His appearance is shaped as he makes his approach:

For the figure they see is from their memory poached.

Not some one unknown - but a Partner-in-crime,

Who steps into focus as he enters their mind.

> **Dimas(adusting his eyes) -**
> **Satan(as Bar-Abbas) :**

Bar-abbas?, is it thou? - hast thou come to this place?

Was thy Amnesty revoked by some added disgrace?

Or hath Sicariian blade pierced thy person at last [13]

---

12 **Dimas / Gestas.**
N.B.1 - Then Pilate commanded Jesus to be brought before him, and spake to him in the following words:
Thy own nation hath charged thee as making thyself a king; wherefore I, Pilate, sentence thee to be whipped according to the laws of former governors; and that thou be first bound, then hanged upon a cross in that place where thou art now a prisoner; and also two criminals with thee, whose names are **DIMAS** and **GESTAS.**
THE GOSPEL OF NICODEMUS OR THE ACTS OF PILATE CHAPTER 6:22-23 (GRYNAEUS - ORTHODOXOGRAPHA, VOL.1, TOM.II, P.643.)

13 When the country was purged of these, there sprang up another sort of robbers in Jerusalem, which were called **SICARII**, who slew men in the day time, and in the midst of the city; this they did chiefly at the festivals, when they mingled themselves among the multitude, and concealed daggers under their garments, with which they stabbed those that were their enemies; and when any fell down dead, the murderers became a part of those that had indignation against them; by which means they appeared persons of such reputation, that they could by no means be discovered. **JOS.WARS.2.13.3.254-255.**

By some family or Roman who still wars with your past?

Satan(as Bar-Abbas) – Dimas:

Hail faithless Dimas, once a brother blood-bound,

Who fought the proud Roman on his conquered ground.

How many the hardships, and what struggles endured;

Oft hounded by enemies and by kindred ignored.

Through many a season waxed we fearless and strong,

But after years of stealth-warfare you claimed we were wrong.

Conviction and conscience caught our company cave-bound;

Demoralized and doubting - our guard had worn down.

Pausing,

What the sword could not kill, you slew with a prayer,

While man after man of our purpose despaired.

It nagged at our heels and it gnawed at our breast;

Yea, the day you deserted Rome made its arrest.

Dimas - Satan(as Bar-Abbas):

I remember those days and the songs on our tongues,

When we fancied ourselves Machabeus' Sons. [14]

But the war that we waged placed our people at stake,

---

14 **Judas Machabeus.**
Then his son **JUDAS**, called **MACHABEUS**, rose up in his stead.
And all his brethren helped him, and all they that had joined themselves to his father, and they fought with cheerfulness the battle of Israel.
And he got his people great honour, and put on a breastplate as a giant, and girt his warlike armour about him in battles, and protected the camp with his sword.
In his acts he was like a lion, and like a lion's whelp roaring for his prey.
And he pursued the wicked and sought them out, and them that troubled his people he burnt with fire:
And his enemies were driven away for fear of him, and all the workers of iniquity were troubled: and salvation prospered in his hand.
And he grieved many kings, and made Jacob glad with his works, and his memory is blessed for ever.
And he went through the cities of Juda, and destroyed the wicked out of them, and turned away wrath from Israel.
And he was renowned even to the utmost part of the earth, and he gathered them that were perishing. **1 MAC 3:1-9.**

Til the cry wasn't freedom, but for killing's own sake.

Pausing,

Speak not Treason to me; 'twas not *I* just released,

Came I not to this cross; will I not hang til deceased?

On the news of thy capture I looked to thy plight,

But I also was taken, though I'd fought my last fight.

Satan(as Bar-Abbas) – Gestas:

His purported intent was not to die with thy friends,

Pointing to JESUS,

But to league with this fool who rejected our ends.

Note well his Love-message; it hath made us Thrice-cursed:

Now the land and the promise are both lost and reversed.

Gestas – Dimas:

Thou abandoned thy comrades for this damn'ed soul,

When oft shoulder to shoulder we fought as a whole?

His preaching defused all popular revolt,

For it fainted men's hearts as it turned out your coat.

Bar-Abbas spake true - thou rebelled against friends,

And your continued beratings undermined our great end.

Your sword wasn't sinless; it still killed and devoured,

Yet in our moment of need, it was sheathed like a coward's.

Dimas – JESUS:

Dost thy dumbness demand *I* be damned and denounced?

Tell them therefore the Truth that they've twisted and trounced.

Not for thee, nor thy message, came I into this Hell,

You were only some rumor - I walked not in *thy* spell...

> **The thieves continue to rail.**
> **Satan(as Bar-Abbas) disappears.**

These vaunts break like thunder rolling off a war-drum,

And like a sheep to be sheared he seems helpless and dumb.

But this tirade must rage till the last breath of life,

When the cursed Beast of Eden provokes his own strife.

PART IV

Satan(Soliloquy):

Now close your dead eyes, and re-visit your pain,

Let thy torment drift Earthwards and awareness regain.

Wake out of this Death-trance, and o'ergaze the dark crowd,

And see Demons and Mortals underneath the same clouds.

From that Death-darkened Void to that Death-darkened world,

By Death's darkened hand into reality they're hurled;

With a quick-jolt of sharp pain their lungs gasp again

As their senses adjust and their thoughts comprehend.

The low-moaning wind lifts the Dimensional-Veil,

Til the Void and the City co-exist in one Pale.

Now clearly, the Malefactors, at last understand,

That the Hell they are in has just linked with their land.

Through that fluttering Veil floats a motley parade:

Gaping-mockers and taunters from that Bottomless-grave.

Through fissures and cracks; (all unseen by our sight),

Issue hot-sparks and foul-smoke as the two Realms unite.

High above the grim-scene, where their Carcasses are hung,

Swarm Legions of Demons flitting about the dark sun.

Their aerial antics, and flocking-sportive displays,

Distract the Un-Earthly from the scene underway.

JESUS - The Women:[15]

B ehold and remember that this day was foretold,

U nderstand with your hearts, be not bitter nor cold.-

T he door of this New-Age shall be closed on the Old.

N ow shall The Accuser be toppled and felled,

O ne Third shall be outcast; from The Heavens dispelled -

T he place where he holds me becomes his locked cell.

Pausing,

F rom this one selfless act, I The Woman re-claim, [16]

O n her true Seed alone shall I bestow my great Name. -

R esurrection shall raise only those without blame.

Sudden pain shoots like fire from his back to his hands,

And on the nails in his feet, like a cripple he stands.

But his legs shake and buckle, and collapse without strength,

As his body falls dangling from his arms at full length.

The spasms that follow are swift and un-checked:

Jactations and wrenchings, (in runaway effect).

These intense violent writhings; (prolonged and sustained),

Will last til the body re-acts not to its pain.

---

15 **JHN 19:25-27.**
16 **GEN 3:15; REV 12:1-6; REV 19:6-9.**

JESUS(after regaining his breath) -
Mary & The Beloved Disciple:

H earken unto me, and consider that which I'll ask,

I n the days of your mourning accept this one task:

M ention why I should suffer, and in Ig-nom-iny die;

S hare the Truth with our Seed; not the Seed that denies,[17]

E ndure and fare well - and care ye one for the other,

JESUS(turning to Mary):

L ament thy Womb not - for thou art always my Mother -

JESUS(turning to The Beloved Disciple):

F rom this moment hence - be her Son and my Brother!

Now the crowd has moved closer to hear the exchange,

As the guards rise in fury, threat'ning all within range.

But The Three forms have sunken back into that space,

Where all Norms are distorted and known-Physics displaced.

---

17 **MAT 13:10-16; MRK 4:10-12.**

PART V

The damned have grown restless, for the Deadline draws near,

And what's coming is certain, but it's outcome unclear.

Here the centuries of planning by the two vying Thrones

Shall decide if this Next Age will be governed or owned.

Satan(as Image-Grotesque) – JESUS:

H ear now my decree, O thou Eunich and Groom, [18]

E xpire not thou yet till your Spouse is foredoomed [19]

W ithin her dead Womb withers what you have sown;

A trophied and shapeless, without form of its own -

S he shall Mother a stillborn sans Husband or Home.

Pausing,

C hoke-out one longing sigh for thy City and Bride;

U nwedded and faithless, she shall lay by my side -

T he Nuptial you've pledged I've disavowed and denied.

O ver thy threshold shall we dance and retire;

F ully embraced, she shall sate my desire -

F rom your bed to my stables she'll be sported for hire.

---

18 This is the Second Acrostic: **He was CUT OFF out of the land of the living: for the transgression of my people was he stricken - ISA 53:8.**
19 **Jerusalem. REV 19:1-9; REV 21-22:1-5.**

O n top of her mount will I multiply my herds;

U n-Menued beasts shall on her Altar be served. -

T he holocaust of hogs shall lure carrion birds.

O pen thy dead eyes and see her future un-wind,

F rom the West comes a man who fulfills my design.

T he Flavian shall come and destroy without pity! [20]

H is Legions shall take and rape thy Wife-City!

E ven so shall he make thy Holies his privy!

Pausing,

L ess than Three Centuries hence; (in the Reck'ning of Time),

A pollo's own King claims my Cross is your Sign. [21]

N icaca shall Counsel; but Rome is more wise, [22]

D esigned like a Phoenix - she shall die and arise.

---

20 **Titus Flavius Caesar.**

21 **Constantine the Great.**

N.B.1 – Eusebius of Caesarea: **CHURCH HISTORY (Book IX, CHAP. 9, PAR. 1-13); THE LIFE OF CONSTANTINE 1.26-31.**

N.B.2 – LACTANTIUS: **ON THE DEATHS OF THE PERSECUTORS, CHAPTER XLIV.**

22 **Nicaea, Bithynia (now Iznik, Turkey).**

N.B.1 - The reference to **'NICAEA SHALL COUNSEL; BUT ROME IS MORE WISE'**, relates not only to the Council of Nicaea(A.D. 325), which attempted to establish; (among other things), the relationship of **CHRIST** to **THE ONE GOD**, but also in a larger degree, to the continuous Spiritual erosion by, and the eventual absorption into The FOURTH KINGDOM 'S Satanic influence **(DAN 7:23-27)** over Rome as the Seat of the Beast - **REV 13:1-2.**

N.B.2 - The concept of a Trinity advances the notion of a Religious Triumvirate, a Romanizing attempt to dethrone the spiritual Oneness within **ELOHIM-the-ONE** with mutual Equality. When JESUS said, **'I and my Father are one'(JHN 10:30),** he was speaking of a spiritual communion that exists whenever the heart of any one within GOD'S creation is perfect or right with GOD'S own heart, i.e., the Ones who keep His Commandments and have the Testimony of JESUS, which is the Spirit of Prophecy - **REV 19:10.**

N.B.3 - The person of the One GOD and his relationship to his Only Begotten Son is clearly understood by the following (and by no means all) Biblical references - **DEU 6:4; PSA 2:7-12; PSA 82:1-8; PSA 110:1-7; ISA 40:18,25; ISA 46:5-10; JHN 10:34-38; REV 2:18; REV 22:9; Etc. AUTHOR.**

O RDO AB CHAO - seed the Womb from the Grave, [23]

F rom the ashes she'll mate, making Kings and Popes slaves. [24]

T iber's Red-Harlot is their flesh and rib-bone. [25]

H er harem of Daughters will their Mother disown. - [26]

---

23 **LAT: ORDER FROM CHAOS.**

24 **Rome / The Papacy.**

In the **Revelation of JESUS CHRIST** it states:

For she saith in her heart, I sit a **QUEEN,** and am no widow, and shall see no sorrow.

Therefore shall her plagues come in one day, death, and mourning, and famine; and she shall be utterly burned with fire: for strong *is* the Lord GOD who judgeth her.

AND THE KINGS OF THE EARTH, WHO HAVE COMMITTED FORNICATION AND LIVED DELICIOUSLY WITH HER, shall bewail her, and lament for her, when they shall see the smoke of her burning, Standing afar off for the fear of her torment, saying, Alas, alas, that great city **BABYLON ,** that mighty city! for in one hour is thy judgment come - **REV 18:7-10.**

AUTHOR.

25 **The Catholic Hierarchy.**

N.B.1 - Even though the '**Donations of Constantine'** have long since proven to be a forgery, the reference to, '**TIBER'S RED-HARLOT IS THEIR FLESH AND RIB-BONE'**, relates to the process of Time in which **KINGS** *have* wedded themselves to **THE HARLOT**, becoming one Flesh and one Mind with her (**CF. GEN 2:21-24 and REV 17:12-14**). In this sense, they have given, and will continue to give to this HARLOT, **THE SIGNET RING** of their Kingdoms, thus corrupting an ever Romanized and Romanizing Papacy into the Seat of the Beast(**CF. the Right hand Signet Blessing with the Right hand Signet Curse: HAG 2:20-23 and REV 13:11-17 respectively**). **SUB-NOTE:** All Satanic imitations are rooted in **ISA 14:12-14.**

N.B.2 - In the **Revelation of JESUS CHRIST** it states:

And there came one of the seven angels which had the seven vials, and talked with me(John), saying unto me, Come hither; I will shew unto thee the judgment of the **GREAT WHORE** that sitteth upon many **WATERS**(i.e., THE TIBER RIVER WHICH FLOWS INTO THE MARE NOSTRUM AND ALL OF IT'S WATERY LINKS):

With whom the **KINGS** of the earth have committed fornication, and the inhabitants of the earth have been made drunk with the wine of her fornication.

So he carried me away in the spirit into the wilderness: and I saw a woman(**THE HARLOT**) sit upon a **SCARLET** coloured beast, full of names of blasphemy, having **SEVEN HEADS** (6 PAST PERIODS OF EMPIRE; 1 FUTURE EMPIRE) and **TEN HORNS** (10 FUTURE KINGS).

And the woman (**THE HARLOT**) was arrayed in purple and **SCARLET** colour, and decked with gold and precious stones and pearls, having a golden cup in her hand full of abominations and filthiness of her fornication: - **REV 17:1-4.**

N.B.3 - The following Scripture indicates that the woman, to whom John is shown, is the *Eternal* city of **Rome / The Vatican:**

And the woman(**THE HARLOT**) which thou sawest is that great city(**ROME**), which reigneth over the **KINGS** of the earth - **REV 17:18.**

AUTHOR.

26 **The Protestant Hierarchy.**

N.B.1 - In the **Revelation of JESUS CHRIST** it states:

And upon her forehead *was* a name written, **MYSTERY, BABYLON THE GREAT, THE MOTHER OF HARLOTS AND ABOMINATIONS OF THE EARTH - REV 17:5.** The above scripture indicates that the woman, to whom John is shown, *is* '**THE MOTHER OF HARLOTS** ', i.e., a **MOTHER** who in turn begets **HARLOT DAUGHTERS.**

E xorcism-vain - they're still Creatures of Rome.

      Pausing,

L ook ye well to this hour, and sign this Concord:

I n lieu of *your* GOD, vow that *I'm* your liege-lord.

V engeance is wrought: a Naught tree for Naught tree;

I n Arcadia come dwell where the ancient one's be.

N ot even *your* GOD will bequeath to the dead,

G ive your birthright to me, that I might reign where he dreads.

Both the damned and the dying within that Void pause,

For this Trophy-of-War could advance their grim cause:

As the blessings of Jacob had been spoiled and lost [27]

So may Heaven's own fortunes be un-done by this Cross.

From the last throes of Death and through faculties dazed;

Physically-drained, but with Spirit un-phased,

His eyes slowly ope, and with the Dragon's they lock,

O'er the bargain that offers his Soul for his Flock.

But what the Dragon beheld, was this Nazarene's vow [28]

N.B.2 - The reference to, **'HER HAREM OF DAUGHTERS WILL THEIR MOTHER DISOWN',** relates to the birth of Protestantism, i.e., The Reformation, which attempted to disown their **MOTHER** by creating a breach, or self-exorcism from The Vatican in A.D. 1517.

N.B.3 - The subsequent religious persecutions, due to the Reformation and counter-Reformation Apostasy(s), testify to The FOURTH KINGDOM'S (Rome's) Satanic influence over both Apostasy(s): i.e.,

And I saw the woman **DRUNKEN WITH THE BLOOD OF THE SAINTS, AND WITH THE BLOOD OF THE MARTYRS OF JESUS:** and when I saw her, I wondered with great admiration - **REV 17:6. AUTHOR.**

27 **1 KNG 11:26-39; 1 CHR 5:1-2; 2 CHR 10:12-19.**

28 **MAT 2:23.**

N.B.1 - The reference to the '**Nazarene 's vow** ' relates to **JESUS** ' life in Nazareth, and his subsequent calling or vow as the **CHRIST**, i.e.:

3480 Nazoraios nad-zo-rah'yos from 3478; a Nazoraean, i.e. inhabitant of Nazareth; by extension, a Christian:--

And that look that defied him was forsworn and unbowed,

And the howl that he vented by this calm-measured slight,

Spread throughout his Dark Legions that filled that dark site.

All their vaunts break like thunder rolling off a war-drum,

And like a sheep to be sheared he seems helpless and dumb.

But their tirades must rage till his last breathe of life,

As the cursed Beast-of-Eden provokes his own strife.

A silence soon settles that un-settles the press,

For an advantage's been lost without word of protest,

And as the deafening stillness echoed into self-doubt,

The last final scene begins to play itself out.

Nazarene, of Nazareth. **STRONG'S CONCORDANCE.**
And **not** to a Nazarite's vow(**NUM 6:1-21**), i.e.:
5139 naziyr naw-zeer'or nazir {{naw-zeer }'; from 5144;separate, i.e. consecrated (as prince, a Nazirite); hence (figuratively from the latter) an unpruned vine (like an unshorn Nazirite):--Nazarite (by a false alliteration with Nazareth), separate(-d), vine undressed. **STRONG'S CONCORDANCE.**
N.B.2 - However, there may be some merit in comparing the separation of a Nazarite with the cutting off of a Messiah(JESUS the Nazarene), as spoken of in the Prophecy(s) of **ISA 53:8** and **DAN 9:26a.**
AUTHOR.

PART VI

Dimas – JESUS:

What mean these strange railings; what links him to you?

These words have dark meanings, they're beyond current view.

Vitriolics like these rage from deep-wounded Hate,

And thy un-yielding stare's but a taunting that baits...

Gestas - Satan(as Bar-Abbas):

In soothe I discern by design thou art guised,

Now un-scale my Third-Eye as to what underlies.

To thy true self revert; that I might see who thou art,

Or is Bar-Abbas co-joined with his Soul's-counterpart?

JESUS – Dimas:
Satan(as Angel of Light) – Gestas:

F or as much as thou seekest to know what transpires,

O nly thou shalt be ware till thou finally expire;

R egard thy erst-comrade and with whom he conspires.

T his pretender seeks lordship o'er Creation's vast sway;

H arming it's Fabric until his hand can be stayed -

E very faction is allied, every Star-World's arrayed.[29]

---

29 **JHN 14:2, JHN 18:36.**

T reason and heresy have shook the GOD-Realms,

R anging and rampant - they'll the Earth overwhelm.

A ges ago - ere your Scribes noted Time,

N ephilim from far took your likeness and kind.[30]

S trong men of renown - as your pre-history tells;

G ods were they called, who in your bloodlines in-dwell.

R epresenting two views - in your fashion and mold,

E ach birthed their own Prophets to petition man's fold.

S ince that Epochal-Fall, the same quarrel has raged,

S preading deeper and further into each culture and age:

I s man to be burdened - like a beast without choice?,

O r shall his will choose which God in whom to rejoice?-

N ow in thy hour of Death let your heart be your voice.

Both pausing,

O bserve and discern who doth inhabit this place:

F allen kings and dominions; all condemned in disgrace.

M ighty heroes lay here; whom the Earth still acclaims,

Y es-ter-day's models, without status or fame.

P roud Dathan and Abiram are consigned to this Hell,[31]

E lam, Tubal, and Asshur in this Nothingness dwell.[32]

O ther clans, long-forgotten, (save by Keepers of Time),

P lunged into this Pit and its boundless confines. -

L ook about and decide, lest the God you have known,

---

30 **GEN 6:1-4; JUD 1:6.**
N.B.1 - 5303 nphiyl nef-eel ' or nphil {{nef-eel '}};from 5307 ; properly,a feller, i.e. a bully or tyrant:--giant.
STRONG 'S CONCORDANCE.
31 **NUM 16:23-35; DEU 11:6; PSA 106:17.**
32 **EZK 32:17-32.**

E xpels your soul here, where all Evil is thrown:

W here their Worm dieth not, is this Condition and State.[33]

A nchored in chains, forged by In-e-luc-ta-ble Fate.

S hades without hope, in this In-term-in-a-ble Wait.

JESUS – Dimas:
Satan(as Angel of Light) – Gestas:

H ereunto have I come - and only I may depart,

E ject all thy doubts and declare whose thou art.

Dimas and Gestas(Soliloquy):

S hunned and alone, I leave this Earth without friends,

T his day I commit to thy purpose and ends.

R egard thy new servant, without malice or hate;

I nto thy Kingdom receive thy humble servant of late.

C ounsel too my last steps, that I may walk in thy light, -

Dimas(indicating Satan):
Gestas(indicating JESUS):

K eep this Imposter away, whom I reject out of sight.

JESUS - Dimas :
Satan(as Angel of Light) - Gestas :

E ven so shall it be, as thy heart hath professed,[34]

N ow prepare to be with me in my Kingdom's rest.

---

33 **MRK 9:44,46,48.**
34 **LUK 23:43.**

PART VII

By mutual exclusion have the sides been declared,

And left only is Death which for a moment was spared.

In one upward thrust; back to their suffering state,

The Three dying corpses hang awaiting their Fate.

The onlookers murmur as the darkness has greyed,

For the light which was blotted streaks forth in long rays.

The guards have just risen, for their orders were clear:

Dispatch the Convicted as the even draws near.

Now devouring Death tears his Soul into shreds,

As his Mouth seeks to form what must be lawfully said.

With his last ounce of courage: (on his heels he is raised),

He commends his Pure-Spirit to the Ancient-of-Days.[35]

Methodically the guards the Three Felons inspect, [36]

But only two barely breathe as the late hour becks.

From one mighty blow both their limbs crack and break,

As they slump-down head-forward, impaled on their stake.

....

---

35 **MAT 27:50; MRK 15:37; LUK 23:46; JHN 19:30.**
36 **JHN 19:31-36.**

The Sho-far's ram's horn blows to start the year's Pasch,

And through the Temple's torn veil the Avenger does pass, [37]

And when the Angel of Death had found naught of Trespass, [38]

I heard an un-earthly rumbling un-earth the Earth's past. [39]

37 **MAT 27:51; MRK 15:38; LUK 23:45.**
38 **EXO 12:23.**
39 **MAT 27:51-53.**